What to do if . . .

The Stork Didn't Leave Instructions

By
Gregory P. Young

How to raise children with
healthy self-esteem

Contact Information:
Greg Young
P. O. Box 67
Centerville, Louisiana 70522
Email: greg.young@cox-internet.com
Website: www.Parents4SelfEsteem.com
Phone: 337-829-9800

Cover design and illustrations by Robert Harris

Contact Information:
Robert "KingRob" Harris
123 Urbana Drive
Lafayette, Louisiana 70506
Email: kingrob@cox-internet.com
Phone: 337-267-3297

ISBN 0-7414-1828-2

Published by:

Six Star Publishing Company, LLC

72 Main Street
Franklin, Louisiana 70538
Toll-free: (866) 786-7550
Fax: 337-828-5542

Printed in the United States of America
Printed on Recycled Paper
Published December 2003

Dedication

This book is dedicated to Janice for being a great partner in helping raise our children. In my opinion, she is one of the best mothers in the world.

To my parents, Karl and Mable Young, for all the love and support they gave me in my upbringing and their continued love and support.

To my three children, Greg Jr., Keith, and Rachael, for the love and joy they bring into my life.

Contents

Foreword

A foreword is customarily written by a famous person. I certainly am not famous, but who better to attest to the success of Greg's parenting skills and philosophy than someone who has taught his three children. I taught Greg Jr., Keith, and Rachael when they were teenagers in the seventh and eighth grades, a most challenging time for adolescents, their parents, and their teachers.

Though each of his children are different in many ways, they all exhibited a healthy self-esteem, a zest for life, and were all well liked and respected by other students and the faculty at school. Each displayed leadership qualities in his or her own way. They were a pleasure to teach, and to be around. All have grown into happy, successful, and productive adults.

This book is not an "untested" theory; Greg's children are a validation that his principles work. I urge you to read this book and apply the knowledge from it to help your children improve their self-esteem!

Janeen F. Robicheaux
Teacher

Preface

What started out as a search for more information to help me become a better parent, became more. The writing of this book has been a much greater project than I envisioned. But then I am an optimist, and I generally underestimate the efforts required in most projects.

Getting this book published for some reason just didn't happen for the longest time. I began writing this book in 1986. There were periods of inactivity due to the pressures of earning a living, being a good parent, spouse, coach, boy scout leader, school board member, teacher, consultant, and filling many other roles.

Even knowing these external reasons for the delay, I would often ask myself was there some other reason why this project was taking so long? Why could I bring so many other projects to a successful completion, yet this one kept dragging on?

I found the answer when I went away for a weekend to a cabin at a state park. This time was for nourishing myself, and I spent the whole weekend alone with nature. It was great. I read the *Celestine Prophecy*, an interesting book with a spiritual theme. It dawned on me that my book had a lot of the practical "how to's" on raising children, but it didn't bring a spiritual awareness to parents.

I believe embracing spirituality as the basis of all other aspects of raising your children is the foundation of being a good parent and helping your children to have healthy self-esteem.

Spirituality is different for each person (I am not talking about religion). Spirituality is knowing that there is a God or Universal Force and that we are connected to this force.

I do not presume to know the best way to help you become spiritual or how to help your children to become spiritual. At best I offer some suggestions for your consideration.

I believe this book can help you with many of the basics of being a better parent. And in this wonderful experience of life, I hope you stay on the path of seeking knowledge and becoming a more enlightened, loving person.

Acknowledgments

This is such a scary page. What if I forgot someone?

Thanks to:

Ralph Morel for starting me on the path to greater self-discovery and understanding human behavior. He was one of the biggest mentors in my life.

Robert Harris for being such a great illustrator.

Amana Shebar for her help in editing, adding ideas, and in helping me to get this book ready for publishing.

Guy Pitts for coming up with the title.

Frances Robichaux for her unwavering support in my life.

Byron Talbot for his support and friendship.

Edith Comeaux for being a wise, wonderful, and joyful teacher.

Sam Jones for his friendship.

Toni Ibert for her support at the end of this project.

Special thanks to GOD for all of the blessings given to me in my life.

Chapter 1

Four Questions

*"The only thing of value we can give kids
is what we are, not what we have."*

Leo Buscaglia

**1. If your children don't get a solid foundation in self-esteem, what kind
of life do you think they will have?**

We know the answer to that question is not good. They will struggle
through life. No parent wants their children to struggle through life.

This book is written to help you make sure that your children do get a solid
foundation in self-esteem so you don't have to answer that first question. It will
provide some answers to the following three questions:

2. How can I help my children have healthy self-esteem?
3. How can I be a better parent?
4. How can I improve my relationship with my children?

1

I want my children to be happy, independent, and well-adjusted individuals who feel good about themselves. All parents want happiness for their children. Many people live their whole lives searching for happiness, never realizing that happiness is an inside job. You can never find happiness in external things, that is, in things outside of yourself. We must realize that we cannot control other people or what they do. Our only control is in how we choose to react to what happens in our world.

To be happy, we must all learn to first find an inner happiness. That is what I believe a healthy self-esteem is -- being happy with yourself, having an inner peace. How can we help our children find an inner happiness?

I believe the following chapters contain some basic things we can do to increase our children's self-esteem, become better parents, and improve our relationships with our children. So where should we start? I believe we should start with....

Chapter 2

Listening To Your Children

*"Nobody cares how much you know until they
know how much you care."*

Anonymous

Listen to your children!! Even when you know they are wrong and you want to correct them for their own good, listen to them first. Nothing validates a person's self-worth like being listened to. You can always have the last word, yet your children should have a chance to express their thoughts and feelings.

One of the most important rules in communicating with your children is not to interrupt them while they are speaking. Let them finish completely before you begin from your point of view. This rule is so important in selling an idea or concept to them. Don't worry, you will get the chance to have your say. We can force our children to be quiet and hear us, but our children will be more inclined to listen to us, if we have listened to them. Try this. It works!

In 1957 I was five and had just learned my first song at school. I was so proud. My aunt came over that evening, and I was excited as I told her that I had learned a new song. I started singing it to her. In the middle of the first verse, she told me that she was tired and did not have time to listen to the song. I still remember my disappointment forty-five years later. My aunt did not realize how proud I was of learning my first song. She probably just had a bad day and was tired. I have used this incident in a positive way over the years. It reminded me to listen to my children when I was tired or when I just did not feel like listening to them.

Think back to the last time someone didn't listen to you. Stop reading right now and remember a specific incident where someone just did not listen to you. How did you feel? Probably not very good. Did you really listen to the other person once you felt they weren't listening to you? Probably not. Remember this the next time your children don't seem to be listening to you. Did you listen to them?

"I never learn anything talking.
I only learn things when I ask questions."

Lou Holtz

This skill of listening can be developed just like any other skill. It takes practice and a conscious effort. Five basic steps to effective listening include:

1. Give the person your total, undivided attention. This means turning off the television, putting the newspaper down, or whatever it takes to give your complete attention to the person speaking.
2. Maintain good, relaxed eye contact.
3. Nod your head to show that they have your attention.
4. Ask good questions when appropriate. This shows that you are paying attention and will improve the quality of the conversation.
5. After they have finished, restate to the other person the major points that you heard. This helps make sure that you are in agreement as to what was said.

ACTIVITY: Take a few minutes to listen to your children NOW. Be genuinely interested and ask good questions such as "What did you do in school today?" ... "What is your favorite subject?" ... "Who is your favorite teacher and why?" ... "If you could do anything you wanted this weekend, what would you do?", etc.

NOTE: Get into the habit of doing things now. Talk with your children today. If they are not available right now, write **"Talk with children"** on a piece of paper and do it tonight or as soon as possible.

Listening intently is often a challenge, and listening to another person when you disagree with them can really be tough. These are times when there is a potential for conflict. So what can we do to avoid or to resolve a conflict? Let's proceed to the next chapter and find out about.....

Chapter 3

Resolving Conflict

"Muddy water let stand will clear."
Chinese Proverb

What you are about to read not only works with children, it works with adults as well. As a consultant and trainer, I have been hired several times to resolve a serious conflict within an organization or company. The key component to solving the conflict is always to really listen to both parties. It is amazing how much a person is willing to work to resolve an issue and how much they will compromise, once they feel that they have really been listened to.

To begin with, never interrupt the person. Let them say everything they want to say. This is usually the first time they have been able to tell their side of the story without having to argue and defend what they want to say. As they talk, you can see their stress level begin to decrease. Their tone of voice becomes more relaxed, their posture changes, and they begin to get in a more receptive state of mind.

Step two involves not making them wrong, even if you feel they are wrong. Coming from a position that forces them to become defensive right away will almost insure that you will not be successful in getting the other person to change. Once you have listened to them without interrupting and you have not made them wrong, then you can begin to present some other information to help them see and hear things in a different light.

Step three is to ask the question, "What can we do to resolve this conflict?" This changes the focus from who is wrong to what can be done to improve the situation.

Finally, even if you still disagree, you can do so with respect for your children's opinion. You can disagree without being disagreeable.

"We find comfort among those who agree with us –
growth among those who don't."

Frank A. Clark

Another method to resolving conflict just involves being more loving. One example that I remember is a conflict I had with my son Keith. As a teenager, he loved playing the stereo in his room so loud that the walls would vibrate. I would arrive home from a long, hard day at work and be greeted with loud music (not my favorite artists either). At first I would march to his room and announce that the music needed to be lowered immediately. He would barely adjust the volume down one level, and then I would come back again. Finally, I threatened to throw the stereo into the bayou behind our house.

I thought about how I could bring about a lasting solution without making him wrong and struggling so much. I decided to try a different approach. I arrived home to the same blaring volume, but instead of demanding that he turn the volume down, I went to Keith and said, "Dad had a rough day at work and would love some quiet time. Would you mind turning the volume down for me?" I then gave him a hug. He didn't just lower the volume, he turned the stereo off! From then on we never had another conflict regarding the stereo. I could just ask in a nice way and he was glad to help me.

*"No man knows his true character until he has run out of gas, purchased
something on the installment plan,
and raised an adolescent."*

Edna McCann

Another secret for getting children (and all people) to change their minds is to use the word….

Chapter 4

Consider

*"You take people as far as they will go, not as far
as you would like them to go."*

Jeannette Rankin

Consider! What a wonderful and powerful word. When you say "you should," "you better," "you have to," the other person doesn't have a choice. I am not talking about areas where you absolutely need to get your children to do things a certain way, such as look both ways before they cross the street.

I am talking about the many areas that you would like your children to do things in a different or certain way. Developing good study habits, getting homework done, and doing chores around the house can often be accomplished with much less force and complaining than we have come to expect.

ACTIVITY: **Think of something you have wanted your children to do. Approach them and ask them to consider doing it. Try it. What do you have to lose? Do it now!**

"We are generally better persuaded
by the reasons we discover ourselves
than by those given to us by others."

Pascal

Let me share an approach that has worked well for me. It follows this format:

1. I decide on the desired behavior and outcome that I want.
2. I communicate this to my children and then listen to all of their reasons why they should not have to do this. This includes how it is unfair, it is hard, other children don't have to do it, and any other reasons they may give.
3. I decide whether any of their reasons make sense and how logical their reasons are.
4. After listening to their feelings, I reconsider the desired behavior and outcome. I then give my children some options or tell them that my original request stands as it was presented. The more importance that I associate with the desired behavior, the less likely I would give them an option. There probably would not be any options on getting in on time for a curfew. There probably would be one or more options on how they go about completing a chore.
5. I give them some time to think about what they will choose and the consequences of their choices.

Once we have agreed upon what is to be done, they generally do it. If they don't do what is agreed upon or what they were told to do, then it is time for the hard part. I am talking about….

Chapter 5

Discipline

*"The thing that impresses me most about America
is the way parents obey their children."*

Duke of Windsor

Discipline is a basic! Without it, no firm foundation for success and happiness can be laid. Children want even-handed discipline, even though they may not know it. Proper discipline shows children that their parents care about helping them. They want their children to become adults who will create a better world for all.

One of the greatest challenges a parent has is to be aware that **disciplining children does not equal punishing them.** I think this point is so important that I want to repeat it – disciplining children does not equal punishing them; rather, **disciplining children is a way to help them establish boundaries and become responsible for their actions.** It helps them to know what is acceptable and what to expect if they cross the line.

Many times while growing up, I remember hating the consequences that I had to face as a result of my behavior. Countless times as an adult, I have thought of my upbringing and thanked God that my parents had the strength to guide me to develop good habits that have served me well.

"Any child can tell you that the sole purpose
of a middle name is so he can tell
when he's really in trouble."

Dennis Fakes

A few critical components in applying discipline are:
- It is important that both parents agree and are **consistent** when applying discipline. Do not discipline them one time and let them off the next.
- **Never discipline your children when you are angry**. Get control of your emotions before applying discipline or setting the consequences.
- Apply consequences with purpose and love (a hug, a smile or a loving comment). Remember that in addition to being loving, you must also **be firm** in disciplining them. Let your children know that you mean business.

"The best cure for anger is delay."

Seneca

I am grateful to my parents for their **discipline with love**. I feel my ability to face tough problems today is a direct result of the fair, unwavering, and consistent application of discipline I received in my upbringing.

The last part of discipline is so important that we will include this as a completely separate subject. I am talking about the need to......

Chapter 6

Separate The Behavior From The Child

*"A torn jacket is soon mended,
but hard words bruise the heart of a child."*

Henry Wadsworth Longfellow

Make sure to separate the behavior from the child when disciplining. **Never** tell a child that he is bad. Always talk about the behavior, not the person. If your child has misbehaved, tell him that his behavior is unacceptable, but he is great! By separating the child from his behavior, you allow the child to do the same. **They learn to not associate behavior with their self-image.**

Focus on the desired behavior more than on the undesirable behavior. This point reminds me of the saying, "What you point a finger at will grow." When two of my children were arguing or fighting, I focused on the behavior that I wanted to see (a loving relationship).

At one time I used to yell. I focused on the undesirable behavior, and a battle would follow. I began to tell my children that they were both good children

12

and that they had a lot of love inside them. Then I would ask them to express more of that loving behavior, and they began to respond more positively.

"The way I see it, if you want the rainbow,
you gotta put up with the rain."

Dolly Parton

It may take telling your children this lovingly and firmly without anger several times before they respond with the desired behavior. Don't expect perfection.

For example, instead of harping on the two D's on their report card, talk about what it will take to get B's in these two subjects on the next report card. Instead of raving about their messy rooms, ask for some specific action that will make the rooms neater, such as "Please make your bed."

Like all behavioral change, this takes time. If the first time you try this, it doesn't produce great results, do not give up. The more you do something, the better you will become at it. It only takes three weeks to develop a habit. The more your children are exposed to positive behavior, the more likely they will begin to model this behavior and change the undesirable behavior. Believe me, this approach works if you are committed to making it work. Remember, a good reward to reinforce positive behavior is recognition and praise.

Let's move on to something that should be so easy to do, but often times it takes a conscious effort, and that is to......

Chapter 7

Express Your Love To Your Children

Express your love to them! I know so many parents who really love their children, but do not know how to express it. They assume their children know how much they are loved. These parents are mistaken. Children need daily reinforcement.

Hug your children every day! A hug and a kiss are free and are two of the most valuable gifts in the world. Everyone needs to feel loved. If at first you or your children are uncomfortable with this show of affection, that is o.k. Hug them anyway. The more you hug them, the easier it becomes. Be a good role model in expressing your feelings. If you have not been an affectionate parent, start becoming one. Touch can heal, encourage, support, and console.

ACTIVITY: Here is a wonderful habit to develop. Every night right before your children go to sleep, tell them "You are a good (boy/girl), I love you, and you can do anything you put your mind to." Start tonight!

14

Imagine if every day of your life you heard that you were a good person, you were loved, and that you could accomplish anything you put your mind to. Don't you think your subconscious mind would have these messages firmly implanted? Of course it would!

Begin expressing your love today! The younger your children are, the better, but it is never too late to start, no matter how old your children are. Do not get discouraged if at first your expression of love is not accepted as well as you would like it to be. Any new habit takes time to develop and become accepted.

Some ideas are often talked about but seldom put into practice. Our next topic is one of these areas. We will address the issue of.....

Chapter 8

Quality Time –
Be Involved in Your Children's Lives

*"What is more important than
sharing time with the people you love?"*

Greg Young

One of the cornerstones of a happy family is that they do things together. Our most precious commodity in this world is our time. If we share that which we value the most with our children, the message they get is that they must be important since we are giving them our time. Be sure to be fully present and not preoccupied when you are with them. Sometimes parents buy material things for their children to show how much they love them. Giving our children our time is so much better than buying material things for them. I believe that the greatest gift is the gift of self.

We hear so much about quality time, but how many of us are able to find a way to spend quality time with our children? One way to develop some quality time is to establish a family calendar. It should be displayed in a central location and list everyone's appointments, sporting events, family activities, school events, business related items, and any other activities. From here we can start scheduling family time together. Once we schedule family time, the chances of it taking place increase dramatically.

A good idea is to have the family eat one meal together each day. The evening meal is a good time to have a family conversation. Have each family member tell how their day went and what is going on in their lives. Don't expect something dynamic -- just good, relaxed conversation. This helps develop a stronger bond between the family members. Do not allow any distractions such as the television or radio.

An important rule is for no one to interrupt the person talking except maybe with a timely question. It might take a little time to train the children (and the adults) to have good listening habits, but it is worth the effort.

Another way to develop quality time is right before bedtime, have your children gather in one bedroom and give each of them a five minute turn to tell the family about their day. Parents should also take a five-minute turn.

Parents need to realize that many of the things their children will tell them may seem insignificant to them. **However, make sure to devote your complete attention to what your children are telling you**. Remember things that seem small to you are significant to them. And if you do not listen to them on the small things now, they will not come to you with their big problems later.

Also, do not feel that you have to give advice on every problem or situation in your children's life. Many times just listening is what they need from you. If you give them answers to everything, you might discourage them from telling you more. If you feel they need some advice, ask before offering it.

A *USA Weekend Magazine* survey on Teens and Self-Image (272,400 teens surveyed) found that parents were rated as the most important influence in their lives. The survey also found that 33% of the teens said that adults don't value their opinion. Remember the listening chapter.

ACTIVITY: This week make it a point to eat a meal together as a family. Remember to leave the television and radio off.

NOTE: The National Center on Addiction and Substance Abuse at Columbia University conducted a study finding that children who never have dinner with their parents have a 70% greater risk of substance abuse.

ACTIVITY: Have a conversation with your children in their bedroom right before bedtime – TONIGHT!

An extension of quality time is for you to be involved in your children's lives. At every age, children need you to be involved in their lives. When they are in school and have school functions, you need to participate with them. Encourage them to join clubs such as 4-H, Cub Scouts, Brownies, Boy Scouts, Girl Scouts, Science Clubs, and team sports. Since participation in team sports can be either one of the best or one of the worst experiences your children can have, we will address this separately in the next chapter.

Being involved sometimes puts added pressure on parents. With a little planning, a balanced life is possible for you and your children. This is an opportunity to teach them how to handle life.

A word of advice – do not join everything! Pick the one or two **things your children enjoy the most, not what you would like them to join**. You will be teaching them how to be a part of the community and helping them learn how to get along with others. Make the commitment. Your children will appreciate and remember this for the rest of their lives.

While we are on the subject of being involved, let's talk about…..

Chapter 9

Team Sports And Achievement In General

"It is easier to live through someone else than to become complete yourself."

Betty Friedan

We need to realize that the skills we now have in handling life took us many years to master and to remember that children are children. They are so impressionable and fragile. They look up to adults, and your actions give them a model of the world.

I coached youth in Biddy Basketball for eight years. It was hard for me to constantly remember that I was dealing with 8 to 12 year-olds. When I started coaching I had been playing basketball for fourteen years. What seemed so simple and easy to me was not simple and easy for them. Even after they had practiced quite a while, they still made many mistakes.

One incident vividly brought this point home to me. During the time I was coaching youth basketball, the National Collegiate Athletic Association (NCAA) finals were being played for the national championship in men's basketball. This particular year, North Carolina and Georgetown were the two teams in the final game. With the score very close toward the end of the game, one of the guards on the Georgetown team made a big goof and threw the ball directly to a North Carolina player. **At that moment**, I realized that if one of the best college players in the nation could make a careless mistake after many more years of practice and playing experience than the children I was coaching, then I needed to be more understanding as a coach of such young athletes. I clearly remember Georgetown's coach John Thompson's reaction to this mistake. He only had praise for his player! From that point on, I was more patient, supportive, and understanding of my young players.

It is important to remember why your children are involved in sports. Coaches and parents must not only tell children the purpose of playing sports, they must also be good role models. I hope your purpose in letting them participate includes:

1. Having fun
2. Learning the fundamentals of the sport
3. Learning about teamwork and how to be a good team member
4. Exhibiting good sportsmanship
5. Putting forth their best effort, and
6. Accepting both victory or defeat with equal grace

Many coaches and parents put tremendous pressure on young athletes. We must be careful how much we expect from our children and how much emphasis we put on winning. The real value is in knowing that you believe in them and their worth, whether they win or lose. Some parents and coaches not only make children feel less than adequate for losing, they **tell** them how inadequate they are. Is this the "reward" our children get for trying as hard as they can?

I remember reading about a survey regarding children's involvement in Little League play. The results were that losing was rated third in the things the children hated the most. Number one was coaches yelling at them, and number two was parents yelling at them!

Parents and coaches have a lot in common. Parents can learn many valuable things from a coach who is aware of his or her awesome responsibility in teaching our youth. With this in mind, I developed the following COACH'S CREED. I hope any coach or parent of young children will read and adopt some of its principles.

Coach's Creed

1. I believe in valuing each young child just as he or she is now.
2. I believe in each child's potential, see that potential, and help him or her to realize it.
3. I believe in the value of teamwork and strive to teach children the joy of working together and the feeling of unity that comes from teamwork.
4. I believe that fundamentals help us to succeed in sports and in life. I teach and have each child practice fundamentals of the game until they are a basic part of the child's skills in that sport.
5. I believe in the value of sportsmanship, I model it, and I reward it.
6. I believe that hard work and being in great physical shape help us to succeed in athletics and in life.
7. I believe having fun is crucial and rewards children for their hard work and efforts.
8. I believe in positive reinforcement and correcting children with kindness and consideration.
9. I believe in valuing and respecting **all children**, not just the athletically gifted ones.
10. I believe in having integrity in dealing with the children, parents, and all others.

Elaborating on each belief...

1. I believe in valuing all young children just as they are now.

   This means unconditional acceptance of all children just as they are -- not waiting for them to become better in order to value and respect them. This leaves out judgment and encourages them to go to the next level to reach their potential. Being treated as valuable helps them to believe in themselves.

2. I believe in children's potential, see that potential, and help them to realize it.

   Your belief can make the difference in what children accomplish and how they feel about themselves. When someone believes in you, it stays with you for a lifetime.

   This principle works. I always believed in my daughter Rachael and her running ability. This belief was given to her from an early age. She needed encouragement to get past what she had set for herself as limits, and I gave it to her. She won more state titles in track than any other girl in the history of Louisiana athletics -- 12 state titles and two state records. Ten years later, she shared with me how she still felt the effects of my belief in her. And at age 50, I still strongly feel the effects of my father's belief in me.

3. I believe in the value of teamwork and strive to teach children the joy of working together and the unity that comes from teamwork.

   We all want to have a feeling of belonging. This is central to everyone. How can we as parents and coaches cultivate this great feeling? What we focus our attention on grows, so if you want teamwork to improve, you must encourage it, give the children opportunities to feel team spirit and reward it when you see it.

   When I was a high school basketball player, I was inspired by one of my teammates. Wayne played so hard that I never wanted to let him down. Whenever I was tired, I would look over at him and see that even though he was tired, he was still giving 100% effort. Coaches should recognize the value in teammates wanting to do better for one another. Team unity helps everyone to be a better player.

   Our country was born from an effort to stand together against the British in the Revolutionary War. This is an example of how powerful teamwork can be. Learning the concepts of teamwork can lead our children to become active participants in the democratic process as adults.

4. I believe that fundamentals help us to succeed in sports and in life. I teach and have each child practice fundamentals of the game until they are a basic part of the child's skills in that sport.

To be a champion, you have to practice like one. All excellence begins with learning the basics of each sport until it becomes a part of you. Sports are much like life in that if you want to take short cuts, you often wind up on the side of the road. Teaching children this concept helps them to become competent and capable human beings.

Every sport has fundamentals that are specific to it. Being in good physical shape, developing your motor skills, and learning successful strategies of the game are some general fundamentals that apply to almost all sports. In life, proper diet, good exercise habits, adequate sleep, effective communication skills, and good mental awareness correspond to fundamentals in sports.

5. I believe in the value of sportsmanship, I model it, and I reward it.

What do we mean by sportsmanship? Being a fair player, helping an opposing player up from the floor or ground, shaking hands after the game, and having respect for your opponents and the officials are examples of sportsmanship. This helps build a better and kinder world.

Teach children that there is no such thing as "losing" if they have done their best. Always believe in their worth, no matter what the outcome of the game is. Teach them to believe in themselves, to be gracious winners, and to have dignity in defeat.

Healthy competition is a positive thing, but being overly aggressive is not. We have all seen examples of too much focus on winning. When an opponent is seen as a hated adversary instead of someone just like you, then you have lost sight of sportsmanship. As a coach or a parent, your behavior is more important than what you say, so model good sportsmanship.

6. I believe that hard work and being in great physical shape help us to succeed in athletics and in life.

"Regular exercise may be the most powerful anti-depressant available."

Michael Murray, M.D.

Who has more energy -- an active and fit person or a person with sedentary habits? We all know the answer to that question, yet many people don't do anything to move from sedentary to active. Teaching our children that **energy is the fuel of life** at a young age serves them well. Children participating in sports get in better physical shape. Exercise helps our bodies to produce endorphins (a chemical that is released into the bloodstream that enhances our immune system, reduces stress, relieves pain, and postpones the aging process). The habit of exercising can provide benefits to us for a lifetime.

Work often brings positive results, whether in youth sports or in adult life. To be a success, one has to learn how to apply oneself to a task. Teaching children this principle shows them how hard work pays off. We all have a sense of accomplishment when we bring something we have worked on to completion. Life rewards us for the right efforts. Being prepared for the demands of life creates its own magic.

7. I believe having fun is crucial and rewards children for their hard work and efforts.

Everyone's soul wants to play. Play creates more energy and frees your child's spirit. Sports are meant to be enjoyable. Laughter can be a result of having fun. It is healing, contagious, cleansing, and promotes unity.

Practice can sometimes become too serious. Be sure to break it up with a fun activity, such as 10 minutes of playing something not related to the sport you are coaching.

8. I believe in positive reinforcement and correcting children with kindness and consideration.

It is easy to give positive reinforcement and recognition to children when they have done a good job. Sometimes they need to improve or change their behavior, and it may be difficult to give positive reinforcement when you need to provide guidance and correct them. Treating them with kindness and consideration increases the possibility that they will apply the guidance you give them and allows them to keep their dignity.

In helping the children to become better players, remember that the goal is **redirection of efforts**, not **criticism of efforts**. Ask yourself, "What are the children learning from my actions and my behavior?" Remember, children are very impressionable. Give them total support and recognition for any efforts that they make after providing guidance to them. The children are more likely to listen to you the next time if you have treated them well.

9. I believe in valuing and respecting **all children**, not just the athletically gifted ones.

Treat all children as VIPs (very important people). By valuing all children regardless of their skill level, you are helping those who have been favored in the past see things differently and those who have been ignored feel important. This increases self-esteem.

Be aware of your behavior when you are dealing with the gifted athlete. Favoritism can be divisive to your team and can be hurtful for the non-gifted athletes.

Coaches yell at the non-gifted athletes more often that they do at their "stars." Yelling criticism or profanity is a demeaning form of communication and is always inappropriate. Yelling encouragement, however, is not only acceptable, it helps build self-esteem!

In choosing children to be on teams, remember that it is better to have a method for team assignment such that no one gets picked "last." From personal experience, I remember the strong emotion of feeling unwanted at the time of team selection. This left a strong impression on my self-image that I had to overcome.

10. I believe in having integrity in dealing with children, parents, and all others.

Whether you are a coach or a parent, **you know when you are coming from a place of integrity**. No one has to tell you. Integrity includes being honest, authentic, and not having hidden agendas or secrecy. Keeping the higher good of all concerned in the forefront becomes your intention. Coming from this place causes you to continually reexamine your attitude and actions. It keeps your awareness level high and models that behavior to the children.

Other activities besides athletics, such as schoolwork, piano, ballet, or anything else your children are involved in, can be important. We can encourage our children to do the best that they can. However, we should not expect perfection and demand that our children become so good in one area that they miss out on one of life's best gifts…**childhood**.

When our oldest child was nine years old, his teacher recommended that he take a test for acceptance in a program for academically gifted students. He took the test and was offered a place in a summer program at a local university about 50 miles from our community. In spite of this, he really wanted to play baseball and would have had to give this up to go to the program. After much discussion between his mother and me and some soul searching, we finally decided to let him play baseball. He was doing very well in school, and we realized that while this was a good program, you are only young enough to play Little League once in your life. If your children are responsible and making good grades, let them have some fun.

Having fun should be a big part of being a child! And speaking of having fun, one way to have fun is to plan...

Chapter 10

Family Outings

*"The best investment you will ever make is
time spent with your children."*

Greg Young

You must plan specific events and schedule them, or your chances of doing things with your family are not very good. Take the time to plan ahead for events or outings with your family, and **schedule them**. Some ideas for your consideration are:

1. Do something as a family one day every weekend (or every other weekend). This can include:
   - A fishing or camping trip
   - Hiking
   - Canoeing
   - Horseback riding
   - Attending sporting events
   - Having a picnic

- Taking a trip to the zoo
- Renting a cabin for the weekend
- Visiting tourist attractions in your area or state
- Visiting the grandparents or other relatives or friends
- Bike riding
- Doing family projects around the house and having a barbecue
- Going shopping
- Visiting museums

The list of things you can do together is almost endless. One of my favorite activities was to get with the children on Thursday or Friday night and look over a state map to pick a town to travel to on Sunday. It did not have to be a large city; most of our trips were to small towns.

You can either reach a group decision or let a different child decide each week. This is an excellent way for you and your family to see your state. Sometimes we would venture into a bordering state. We brought sandwiches and drinks with us and had a picnic. It really does not cost much for such an outing.

2. Make one week night "family night" each week. As a family, do something together such as:
- Watch a movie on television or watch the Discovery Channel
- Rent a video cassette, dvd, or go to the movies
- Dine out
- Play games
- Have a family conversation
- Go riding in your car
- Put a puzzle together

"The best things you can give your children next to good habits, are good memories."

Sidney J. Harris

Here is another opportunity to get into the habit of following through. **Stop reading this book long enough to plan a family outing**.

TAKE A FEW MINUTES RIGHT NOW!

ACTIVITY: Plan and schedule a family outing.

Let's now turn to a subject that at one time or another probably concerns every parent, and that is…

Chapter 11

Your Children's Friends

Although you cannot pick and choose your children's friends, you can encourage them to associate with children that you know have a good, strong family background. Again it helps to remember that adults aren't perfect, and certainly children aren't perfect either. Do not make your children feel wrong in their judgment of a friend, or they will defend their feelings toward that friend. I remember in junior high school, we would sneak around to see another friend we really liked. Chances are your children will sneak around also, if you try too hard to force your choice of friends upon them.

When dealing with the issue of friendships, it might help to review chapter two on **listening**. If you listen to your children first and then explain why you do not want them to hang around with this certain person, they will be more likely to follow your advice. When disagreeing with your children, if you tell them the reason you made that particular decision was because you love them, they will accept it better than if you tell them they have to do it "just because" you said they must.

Sometimes my children would tell me they wished I did not love them quite so much. But I know there are some positive aspects of telling them the "why" of some difficult decisions we have to make as parents. **And love for them is the main reason for our decisions**. I think it is important for them to know that.

*"The only way to make a man trustworthy is to trust him,
and the surest way to make him untrustworthy
is to distrust him and show your distrust."*

Henry Lewis Stimson

One other thing on friends; if your children have a friend you wish they did not have and you have not been able to change that friendship, make the best of it. Try to be a positive influence in that other child's life by including him in selected activities to show that you accept him. Many children with "bad behavior" are really looking for any kind of attention. With some help, they may learn to change their negative behavior to positive behavior and then may receive some positive attention.

One area that usually doesn't get much positive attention is…

Chapter 12

School Homework

Someone needs to regularly monitor your children's homework and progress at school. Do not wait until report card time. With both parents working in many cases, it can be a shared responsibility. Rule number one is...

DO NOT DO THEIR HOMEWORK FOR THEM!

Children are very good at getting a parent to do their homework for them. "I can't find the answer to this question in chapter 2," is an old line that can be effective if we are not aware. Before you know it, you are looking up all the answers. One of my favorite comments to our children was "Your mother and I already have diplomas, and we do not need to earn another one."

A helpful tip to get homework done is to give your children the first 30 minutes to an hour after school to enjoy themselves and unwind. After that period, get them in the habit of doing their homework first before anything else. Help them to form good habits. Consistent effort for a month or two will establish a habit. Another good rule is no television or radio on while doing homework (unless it is classical music, which has been found to improve mental alertness). Teach them the value of establishing good habits.

Another thing you could consider that will serve them well later is…

Chapter 13

Jobs For Your Children

"If you want children to keep their feet on the ground, put some responsibility on their shoulders."

Abigail Van Buren

Teach your children to work! This area is somewhat like discipline in that we may find it takes some effort, but it is critical. Give your children some chores at home, even when they are young. It can be simple things such as:
- Making their beds each day
- Picking up their clothes
- Keeping their room straight

As they get older, you can gradually add other jobs such as:
- Folding clothes
- Washing the dishes
- Sweeping
- Mopping
- Cleaning their bathrooms
- Washing the car
- Taking the trash out

On jobs such as cutting grass, make sure they are old enough and impress upon them the need for safety around lawnmowers.

Remember, do not overdo this. Children should not be slaves. Give them a moderate amount of work considering their homework situation, extracurricular activities, and so on.

ACTIVITY: Think of jobs appropriate for your children considering their age. Make a list of chores and discuss it with your children. Remember that working will help them to develop responsibility.

"The greatest ability is dependability."

Curt Bergwall

Once your children are teenagers, you may want to consider encouraging them to find a part-time job outside of the home. This will give them some spending money, help increase their self-esteem, and teach them how to be good employees. As an extra side benefit, it may help them appreciate what you have to go through in the work world.

You may want to consider getting them to save some of their earnings while having the rest to spend. Teach them to save. We will have a chapter on teaching your children about money later. This is such a wonderful habit to help them develop!

Here are 8 tips for your children on how to get a job:

1. Be neat in appearance when going to a job interview or putting in an application.
2. Fill out the application thoroughly, neatly, and accurately. Be sure to include your phone number.
3. Follow-up after putting in an application.
4. When on a job interview, ask good questions, such as:
   - "What is important in this job?"
   - "What qualities are you looking for in the person you want to hire?"
   - "What is important in this company?"
5. Listen to what the prospective employers tell you. Then tell them why you would do a good job.
6. Show them that you want the job! Be enthusiastic and eager.
7. Do not just put in one or two applications. Fill out plenty of applications. The more applications you fill out, the better the chances of getting a job.
8. Finally, utilize all resources, including people your parents know, to help you get a start.

NOTE: I remember clearly when I went to apply for my first job over 30 years ago. The manager, Mr. Barnes, told me there weren't any openings and that they were not hiring. I went home and told my father, expecting that to be the end of it. I was wrong. My father gave me some valuable advice. He told me to go back every three days, and being very polite, to ask if there was an opening. I did that for several weeks, and finally came by when another boy had just quit. I got the job and worked there for the next four years until I graduated from high school. The valuable lesson my father taught me was **positive persistence pays off**! So encourage your children to keep trying until they are successful.

Now we are ready to address two subjects that are often touchy, but are so important, the first one being…

Chapter 14

Sex And Your Adolescents

The United States continues to have one of the highest teenage pregnancy rates in the developed world—twice as high as those in England, Wales or Canada and nine time as high as rates in the Netherlands and Japan.[1]   A sexually active teenage girl who does not use contraception has a 90% chance of becoming pregnant within a year. [2]   Make sure to have a conversation about sex with your children when they reach adolescence. Do not let them learn about sex from their peer group. So much misinformation is taught in this manner that there is a real danger that your children will not have correct information to make informed decisions. You can't afford to wait. By their 18th birthday, 60% of teenage women and nearly 70% of teenage men have had sexual intercourse.[3]

---

[1] AGI, *Teenage Sexual and Reproductive Behavior in Developed Countries: Can More Progress Be Made?*, New York, AGI, 2001

[2] Alan Guttmacher Institute, *Sex and America's Teenagers*, 1994

[3] Alan Guttmacher Institute, *In Their Own Right: Addressing the Sexual and Reproductive Health Needs of American Men,* New York, AGI, 2002; AGI, unpublished tabulations of the 1995 National Survey of Adolescent Males; and AGI, unpublished tabulations of the 1995 National Survey of Family Growth

If you are not comfortable discussing this subject with your children, at the very least find a way to get them some information. You may want to go to your local bookstore and find an acceptable book to buy. Most of these books are factual and some have explicit illustrations. Since there are a wide range of value systems, **be sure to preview any book before giving it to your children** and look for one that you feel comfortable with.

Even though you give them good information, I still think you need to communicate to them how you feel about sex. Let them know that sex is o.k. at the right age and in the right circumstances. You fill in these details according to your belief system. Help them to understand that it is normal for teenagers to begin to feel a natural biological urge and to be curious about sex. Make sure they know these feelings are normal, **yet actions are the real area for concern**. They need to realize that sex is one area where responsibility for their actions can last a lifetime (and can even shorten their lifetime)! *Every year, roughly 4 million new sexually transmitted disease (STD) infections occur among teenagers in the United States.*[4]

As parents, we are faced with some serious decisions regarding teenage sex. Never before has there been so much peer pressure to have sex at a young age. There is so much exposure to sex on television, in music, and in the media. We all must answer tough questions such as "Would you talk to your son or daughter

---

[4] AGI, *Teenage Sexual and Reproductive Behavior in Developed Countries: Can More Progress Be Made?*, New York, AGI, 2001

about the importance of using condoms, or would you feel that if you did, they would see this as giving them permission to have sex?"

There are no fast and easy rules. My advice is for parents to discuss these issues with each other and agree on what they feel is best. Then communicate this to your children, and believe that you made the right decision.

One final thought on this subject. Do everything you can to help them feel good about the changes their bodies are going through. If your children are one of the first to physically mature or one of the last to mature, they may need some reassurance that they are normal and that their bodies are fine just the way they are. This advice is partially from my own experience as a boy. As a young teenager, I was one of the last boys in my class to physically mature, and I remember the dread of taking a shower after physical education classes. So give your children reassurance that at whatever rate their bodies are changing, it is natural and normal.

The second touchy subject we will cover is...

Chapter 15

Respect Your Child's Right To Privacy

Trust, respect, and heart-to-heart communication are keys to developing a relationship with your children that support honesty and openness. This issue also touches on control vs. guidance. Control is effective as long as the "controller" is present. Guidance is effective for the long haul and can help your children resist peer pressure.

Snooping creates separation between yourself and your children and may cause them to think of you as invasive and suspicious. The consequences of snooping may lead them to fear you and experience shame about your perception of them.

Do not ever go through your children's wallet or purse. Let their room be their private domain. Whatever good you may do by finding out something by prying behind your child's back will be more than offset by violating his or her basic need for privacy and the trust between you.

If you suspect your children might be experimenting with drugs, remember the eyes are windows to possible drug use. Pay close attention to their eyes for an early sign. Are they looking at you, or does it seem like they have something to hide?

A possible sequence to follow in looking for probable drug use would be to look for signs of:

- Apathy
- Withdrawal
- Hostility
- Radical change in behavior
- Moods swings
- A different peer group
- Changes in personal appearance
- Dullness, redness or irritation of the eyes
- Dilated or fixed pupils
- A change in habits, such as late nights or sleeping more than they normally do

Possible drug use calls for heart-to-heart conversation, not searching for evidence. Give your children a chance to be honest with you. The more you put them on the defensive, the less chance of honesty you have. Be direct without threatening them.

Only after dialogue has failed should more aggressive measures be considered, such as school bags, closets or room searches. Again, **I would like to emphasize that the decision to search through their room or belongings should not be made lightly**. If they know that you have invaded their privacy, you might lose their trust and may cause them to feel less worthy ("My parents don't trust me"). So give this area some serious thought before taking action.

On a less serious note, you have the right to demand how they keep their room, but compromise is possible. Within your guidelines, this is one area where it is possible to allow them a little independence without giving up too much. Good habits in housekeeping are valuable. However, the sense of pride children can get from decorating and arranging their rooms and from having a place of their own is important. Everyone needs a little "space" to retreat to. If their room doesn't meet your standards, try closing the door!

Our next chapter is about a character trait that small children have in abundance. However, adults soon begin to condition children and reduce their...

Chapter 16

Creativity

"Discoveries are often made by not following instructions, by going off the main road, by trying the untried."

Frank Tyger – *Forbes* Magazine

The most important component necessary for creativity to be present is **lack of criticism**. Most children tested between the ages of 2 and 4 years old were very creative, but by the time they reached the age of 7, only a small percentage of these same children were still very creative. This difference is due to parents, teachers, and other adults telling the children to stop asking questions. "Just do as I tell you to do." Parents begin conditioning children to be just like everyone else.

Encourage your children to use their imaginations. Buy games for them that stimulate creativity. Ask them to tell you a night time story. Don't laugh at their efforts. Help them feel comfortable in trying new things. Loosen up and try being more creative around them. Do things together that require some creativity. And finally, substitute **encouragement** for criticism.

ACTIVITY: Tell your children a bedtime story tonight. Ask them if they want to tell you a make believe story. Encourage them to be creative.

ACTIVITY: Give your children a pad and pencil and ask them to draw a feeling, such as love, pain, excitement, or to write one paragraph on how people get rich. Use your imagination and come up with an idea to get them thinking creatively.

It is time to cover another part of parenting that is difficult for most parents to handle. But as with most difficult areas, it is crucial to raising strong and independent children. The next chapter is about…

Chapter 17

Independence / Allowing Your Children To Fail

"For many, life's longest mile is the stretch from dependence to independence."

Carla B. James

Most people can handle the first part of this subject (independence), but they never realize without the second part (allowing your children to fail), children cannot become independent. I am not advocating that you encourage your children to fail -- only that you **allow** them to fail.

"Victory is sweetest when you've known defeat."

Malcolm Forbes

Teach your children that failure often forms the foundation for success. Many successful people experienced hardships and early failures that better prepared them for greatness and success. Some examples are:

- Walt Disney was fired because he had no good ideas.
- Beethoven was told by his music teacher that he was "hopeless" as a composer.
- Thomas Edison was told as a boy by his teachers that he was too stupid to learn anything.
- Einstein was four years old before he could speak and seven before he could read.
- Sidney Poitier was rejected in his first audition at the American Negro Theatre.
- Dustin Hoffman was rejected four times from the Actor's Studio before finally making it through.
- Hank Aaron and Babe Ruth struck out more times than any other players in major league history.

And finally one of our greatest presidents, Abraham Lincoln, had the following failures:

- Failed in business more than once
- Had numerous personal setbacks, such as his sweetheart dying and his having a nervous breakdown
- Defeated in elections for public office five times
- Defeated for various party nominations, including Vice-President before he was elected President of the United States

This subject reminds me of the story of a little girl who saw a butterfly struggling to free itself from its cocoon. She felt sorry for it and freed the butterfly from the cocoon. However, the butterfly soon died. It needed to develop its strength by working itself out of the cocoon. Even with her best intention, the girl hurt the butterfly by trying to help it too much.

The desire to help our children over every rough bump is strong, but they must learn how to handle the bumps. When they are adults, life will give them some bumps to handle. If they do not have any experience as children in going through some rough spots, then they will not know how to handle them as adults.

One area where parents often become involved too quickly is in matters involving teachers. I only went to my children's schools four times in the 16-year period my children were in school. Yet I know many parents who are at school attacking teachers and defending their children several times every year! These same parents accept the excuses their children give them as to why they make bad grades in Ms. Smith's class; yet I have seen these children riding their bikes from 3:15 p.m. until darkness every day. I wonder why the parents aren't encouraging these children to study more.

Unless it was a really unfair situation, I expected and demanded that my children made good grades (no excuses were accepted), and they did. Each parent sets his or her own standards as to what constitutes "good grades". I think this approach is valuable because if your children go on to college, they **will** have some teachers who will make passing as difficult as possible. Also, handling difficult situations can help them to become more independent.

"Only when a tree has fallen can you take the measure of it.
It is the same with a man."

Anne Morrow Linbergh

Helping children grow from total dependence to independence is one of the responsibilities of parenthood and should be a gradual process. The need for control from a parent is high for three-year old children. However, as children get older, it is important to begin gradually loosening the control, so that by the time they are 17 or 18 years old, they are independent. Do not wait until they are graduating from high school and then give them their independence all at once.

This usually does not work and is not fair to the young adult. Graph 1 illustrates this point, while Graph 2 illustrates a more desirable approach.

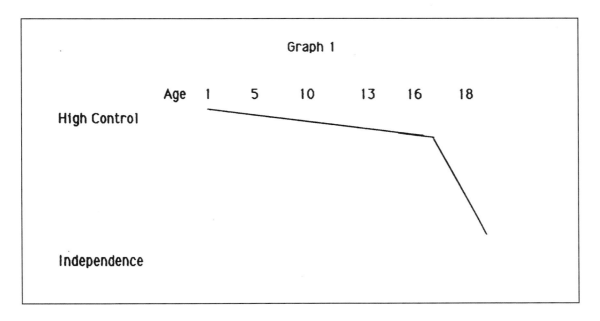

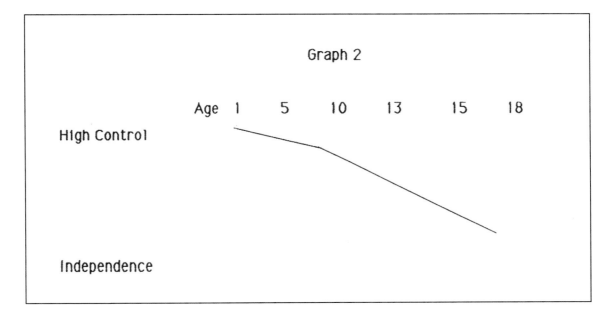

Give your children support, reinforce their individual worth as a person, and encourage their efforts. Let them know that failure is a part of life and often it is a big part of success. Help them to see that there are lessons to be learned from their failures. It is not failure if you have done your best. Teach your children to do their best, accept the outcome, and learn valuable lessons from each endeavor.

Most people who accomplish great things do not give excuses when things do not go well. They accept the responsibility to make things better. **Teach your children that excuses are a poor substitute for success**.

The next chapter is about an area that can help your children in developing independence and experiencing success both now and throughout their lifetime. This area is…...

Chapter 18

Teaching Your Children About Money

Do you want your children to struggle with money issues when they are adults? Do you struggle with money issues now? If so, I suggest that you buy one or two good books on money management and begin to make improvements in that area of your life. I could probably write a book on that subject from my life experiences. I was financially successful at a young age, then made some poor decisions, struggled financially for a few years, and then once again became financially successful.

A statistic that jumped out at me was that *79% of students have never taken a course on personal finance in school.*[5] Our children need some education in this area. Here are some basic truths to teach your children so they will begin developing good habits and a solid foundation for becoming financially successful.

Principle 1 – It is not how much you make, it is how much money you spend in relation to how much you make. Some people amass fortunes without ever making a great deal of money, and others earn tremendous salaries and are actually "broke."

Have your children save a part of every dollar they earn or receive. This is the single most important principle in my opinion. I highly recommend that you buy a wonderful piggy bank, "Money Mama", invented by Lori Mackey. It teaches your children how to save 10% for their future, invest 10% to build their fortunes, and give 10% to a charity of their choice. The remaining 70% is for them to spend. To order Money Mama, go to **www.prosperity4kids.com**.

Once your child has $25.00 saved, bring him or her to a bank and open a savings account. Once he has over $100.00 in the bank, open an account with a solid mutual fund for him. If you have a trusted financial advisor, consult with him or her. If you don't have one, ask your friends to refer one to you.

---

[5] The 1999 Youth and Money Survey was sponsored by the American Savings Education Council (ASEC), the Employee Benefit Research Institute (EBRI), and Mathew Greenwald & Associates, Inc. The survey was underwritten by the TIAA-CREF Institute, an ASEC Sustaining Partner.

If I had just saved 10% of every dollar I made, I would have been able to retire already. Time is not forgiving when it comes to saving and investing. Just ask anyone who starts thinking about saving for retirement at age 45 or 50. On the other hand, if someone starts saving for retirement in their early 20's, he is basically home free.

Principle 2 – Be a good role model when it comes to how you handle money. *USA Weekend Magazine in partnership with* **Channel One***, the in-classroom news program, surveyed 193,224 students in grades 6-12. When completing the statement "I've learned a lot about money matters from:" 77% checked "A parent".*[6]

In a smaller study of 1,000 students interviewed by telephone in the 1999 Youth and Money Survey, *94% of students say they are likely to use their parents as a financial information source.*[7] Realize that **you are the major source of your children's education in regards to money**. So if you are not sure they should be learning from you in your current financial state, make the commitment to yourself to start improving your money management skills. If not for yourself, do it for your children.

Principle 3 – Teach them how to make money. It can be simple ways such as babysitting, cutting a neighbor's lawn, washing cars, cleaning houses, or doing chores around the house. Encourage them in finding ways to do this, even when they are young. A six-year-old can find a way to make a dollar if you believe they can. Teach them the secret to making money -- finding a need and filling it.

Activity: Challenge your children to find a way to make $5.00 or $10.00 in the next week. Then get them to save some of it.

Principle 4 – Teach them about the dangers of credit cards. Warn them about the ease in which credit card companies entice us to live beyond our means and mortgage our future. Only a small percentage of people use credit wisely. Even if you aren't currently practicing what you preach, preach anyway, and resolve to become smarter in your use of credit cards.

---

[6] USA Weekend Magazine, Channel One
[7] The 1999 Youth and Money Survey was sponsored by the American Savings Education Council (ASEC), the Employee Benefit Research Institute (EBRI), and Mathew Greenwald & Associates, Inc. The survey was underwritten by the TIAA-CREF Institute, an ASEC Sustaining Partner.

Activity: **If you owe money to credit card companies, develop an action-plan to reduce your spending, which will start reducing your debt. Make a concerted effort to eliminate credit card debt. Start doing this today.** I highly recommend an audio program by John Cummuta, *Transforming Debt into Wealth*. You can find this and other programs on building wealth at www.peoplesuccess.com/conant.htm

If you have more than one child, the next chapter is of utmost importance. It is about…

Chapter 19

Accepting The Differences In Children

*"The whole problem of life is to
understand one another."*

Woodrow Wilson

Have you ever heard, "Why can't you be more like your brother or sister?" What a negative reinforcement! This message conveys that the child is not adequate as he or she is. What we want to say is the **behavior** of the other child is more acceptable to us.

The next sentence is probably the **MOST** important sentence in this whole book. **Please read it several times**.

**The most critical thing necessary to improve a
child's self-esteem is to accept them as they are now!**

"But that is hard!" you might say. Well, I know from first hand experience that it works. Until you accept any person as he or she is, they will not begin to improve in a lasting way.

This is not to say that you do not want the child to behave differently. Look for the good in the child and compliment him on it. Recognize your children's accomplishments and appreciate their differences. For example, our three children all excelled in different areas. Greg Jr. excelled in academics, Keith in basketball, and Rachael in distance running in track and field.

Show some genuine unconditional love. So what is unconditional love? It is just what the words mean. I love you with no conditions attached. I may not love your behavior, but YOU are great! Always make that distinction! **Always love the child.**

Realize that all people are different. An outgoing child and a reserved child are both perfect as they are. Do not attempt to get the outgoing child to be more reserved or vice versa. Accept them as they are. Make every effort not to judge your children. Help them feel good about the way they are. If and when they want to change, **then** offer support and encouragement. This will become permanent change only if **they** want it.

Grades in school are often one area in which parents compare children. If you must compare, compare effort and not grades. All children have different capacities to learn and process information. Remember those magic words **encouragement** and **support** when dealing with your children. In his book **Unlimited Power**, Anthony Robbins sheds some light on the different ways children process information. He relates some success he was able to help students achieve by simply using different approaches. The book is about Neuro-Linguistic Programming (NLP). I recommend it to anyone interested in improving their ability to communicate and relate more effectively with others.

ACTIVITY: Have your children make a Success List. A Success List is simply a list of things they have accomplished, or reasons why they feel good about themselves. It should be posted where they can see it every day. You could also make a list for them as to the good qualities that you see in them.

This chapter gave you an important challenge – to accept the differences in children. The next chapter will help you in…

Chapter 20

Understanding The Differences
In Children

What makes children from the same family raised in the same house by the same parents, so different? No book can fully answer that question. However, we will give you some information to help you better understand the differences in your children's behavior, and we can provide some insights into how to deal more effectively with the different behaviors your children will exhibit.

These next few chapters will explain four basic types of behavior I learned about from a profile instrument that is no longer in use. I received permission from the profile publishers to use their information here. Be aware that children may exhibit more than one of these behavior types. Usually though, they will have one behavior that is more dominant than the others.

The four types of behavior are:
- Direct
- Influencing
- Steady
- Correct

The next chapter will give you some insight into…

Chapter 21

Understanding Children
With Direct Behavior

*"If you have anything of importance to tell me,
for God's sake begin at the end."*

Sara J. Duncan

The first type of behavior we will discuss is easy to recognize. It is direct behavior. We all have seen children who are demanding, tell you what they want, are impatient, and can sometimes be difficult to deal with. We often look at the negatives associated with this type of behavior. If we learn how to help them maximize their strengths and minimize their weaknesses, these children have many positives. How can we do this? By learning more about what motivates them and what we can do to positively interact with them.

Some clues to recognizing this behavior in children include:
- Being direct / demanding
- Telling people what they want
- Being competitive
- Being impatient
- Being results oriented
- Being persistent

- Going at a fast pace
- Being more task oriented than people oriented

What motivates these children? Some things that motivate them include:
- Giving them as much **freedom** as possible
- Showing them how to get the results they want in a positive way
- Giving them challenges
- Being direct with them
- Recognizing their accomplishments
- Giving them opportunities to be a leader
- Letting them proceed with things at a faster pace
- Having fewer rules (only the most important rules)
- Getting right to the point when talking to them

What happens when we help these children to feel good about themselves and be more aware of how their behavior affects others? Children with direct behavior who feel good about themselves may then be perceived as leaders who make quick decisions and are not afraid to take risks. They like challenges and will work to get results in any project they undertake. They do get results!

What happens when children with this behavior do not feel good about themselves and are not aware of how their behavior affects others? They can be perceived as bullies who are stubborn and who undermine teamwork and the overall good of the group. They may be seen as the rule breakers and troublemakers. Sometimes teachers, parents, or other adults may say these children are in danger of winding up in trouble with the law.

Yes, the power of expectations: understanding our children's behavior and their own self-esteem all are so important in guiding our children into the future we want for them. Please make sure that you talk positively about your children and recognize their good qualities. And remember, when you want to correct their behavior, talk about the behavior and not the child.

Now let's continue with…

Chapter 22

Understanding Children
With Influencing Behavior

The second type of behavior we will discuss is also fairly easy to recognize. It is influencing behavior. Children with this behavior tendency are very verbal and almost constantly seek attention. "Are we having fun yet?" could be their motto. They can talk almost non-stop and sometimes are loud. They tend to be optimistic by nature and are generally happy children.

Some clues to recognizing this behavior include:

- Wanting to be the center of attention
- Acting animated
- Talking almost constantly
- Having a high energy level
- Going at a fast pace
- Being people oriented
- Wanting to have fun
- Trouble concentrating very long on one task
- Liking a change of pace (gets bored easily)
- Not liking rules
- Squirming if required to stay still too long

What motivates these children? Some things that motivate them include:
- Giving them **recognition**
- Finding ways to make work fun
- Having fewer rules
- Having some breaks in any task that takes more than 30 minutes
- Giving them hugs often
- Giving them projects that encourage creativity

Children with this behavior who feel good about themselves can be perceived as leaders with social skills who can help everyone feel better and get along together. They help to create enthusiasm, and their energy is contagious.

When children with this behavior do not feel good about themselves and are not aware of how their behavior affects others, they are sometimes thought of as the class clown or the goof-off, someone who is not serious about doing well in school or in tasks given to them.

We continue with...

Chapter 23

Understanding Children
With Steady Behavior

The third type of behavior we will discuss is steady behavior. Children with this behavior tend to blend in. They follow the rules, prefer a steady pace, like a stable environment, and do not like change. They have the most flexible behavior and look for ways to fit in.

Some clues to recognizing this behavior include:

- Being somewhat talkative in a quiet manner
- Being shy until they know you
- Preferring the safe and known (they are not risk takers)
- Liking and following rules
- Fitting in well with a group
- Being both people oriented and task oriented
- Being able to sit still

Some things that motivate children with steady behavior include:

- Showing sincere appreciation
- Treating them **fairly**
- Telling them what is expected, preferably in writing
- Checking with them often to see how they are coming along on a task

- A structured environment
- Going at a slow and steady pace
- Explaining things thoroughly

Children with steady behavior that feel good about themselves can be perceived as team players. These children are hard workers who are almost always dependable. They help get the task done without a lot of complaining, and you can count on them.

When children with steady behavior do not feel good about themselves, they are sometimes perceived as weak, indecisive children who can be easily led. They may be taken advantage of unless they receive help in establishing boundaries.

And finally….

Chapter 24

Understanding Children
With Correct Behavior

*"It is surely one of nature's jokes
that she so often gives an abundance of
self-confidence to those who are not analytical
and withholds even a smidgen of it
from those who are."*

Patricia Pumphrey

The fourth type of behavior we will discuss is correct behavior. Children with the correct behavior tendency are concerned with how they look in other's eyes. They strive to do things perfectly! They want things organized and above all, everyone must follow the rules.

Some clues to recognizing this behavior include:
- Having good analytical skills
- Following the rules and directions to the "t"
- Being quiet
- Asking a lot of questions
- Taking longer to finish projects (because they want it to be perfect)
- Being critical of others' efforts
- Being neat and organized

Some things that motivate children with correct behavior tendency are:

- Commenting on the quality and accuracy of their work
- Explain things to them **logically**
- Providing them with complete instructions (preferably in writing)
- Allowing them sufficient time to complete the assignment
- Setting a deadline on assignments to encourage completion
- Making sure everyone follows the rules when they are involved
- Staying focused on one task at a time
- Present evidence to support your point of view
- Giving them the opportunity to ask questions
- Responding positively to their questions

Children with correct behavior who feel good about themselves can be perceived as efficient and well-organized thinkers. They are the people to go to if you need answers to a tough problem. People respect their analytical ability and their calm, "under control" manner.

When children with correct behavior do not feel good about themselves, they can be perceived as critical nitpickers, who complain about everything. Nothing is ever good enough. They can become like those who never enter the game, but always sit on the sidelines and criticize those actually playing. Fear of making a mistake can keep them from doing anything.

"Unless a capacity for thinking
be accompanied by a capacity for action,
a superior man exists in torture."

Benedeeto Croce

And now for …

Chapter 25

A Summary:
Understanding The Differences
In Human Behavior

*"When we treat a man as he is,
we make him worse than he is.
When we treat him as if he already
were what he potentially could be,
we make him what he should be."*

Goethe

These last few chapters have just touched the surface on the subject of human behavior. I hope they have given you some insights into how to more effectively deal with children having different behaviors. By being aware of what your and your child's behavior styles are, you can recognize what needs to be done to improve your communication. This information was critical in helping me turn a strained situation with my older son into the positive relationship we have now.

An overview of the problems we experienced when my son was four or five years old follows:

My behavior tendencies are influencing and direct in that order. His behavior tendencies were correct and steady. I was very emotional and direct in dealing with him, and he was uncomfortable with this approach. He was an analytical (not emotional) child, and he did not like directness, but preferred a softer approach.

I pressed harder and harder to get him to be happy and optimistic. The message he was getting was, "You are not o.k. as you are." My mistake was in believing that since I was happy and optimistic, by being outgoing and emotional, for him to become happy and optimistic, he needed to be more like me. **What a mistake!**

Fortunately, I experienced some corporate training on team building at this time. The instructor, Ralph Morel, described some instruments that identified children's behavior tendencies. It included information on how to effectively deal with each behavior. When my older son took the profile, it showed the "expected" behavior was exactly the same as my profile! But the "this is me" behavior was directly opposite from mine. I felt like I had been blind and someone had given me the precious gift of sight! From that point on, our relationship improved to where now I am proud and content with our relationship. It is everything I could have hoped for.

Let me give you one example of the good that can come from finding out more about your children's behavioral tendencies. Research has shown that normally (there are always exceptions) children with the best self-image are those with direct behavior. The children with the next best self-image are those with influencing behavior, followed by children with correct behavior, and normally, children with the weakest self-image are those with the steady behavior. This type of information can be helpful in alerting you to the need to spend a little extra time with those children who may have a weaker self-image.

In the field of education, our teachers could benefit from this information. Anyone can teach children with steady or correct behavior tendencies. The challenge is in teaching the more active children with direct and influencing tendencies who have shorter attention spans.

In closing, please learn as much as you can about human behavior. There are many avenues to obtaining this information. Local universities and libraries can be good resources.

Now we will cover what I believe to be the basis of all aspects of conscious child rearing, and that is...

Chapter 26

Having A Spiritual Connection

"My religion is very simple. My religion is love."

Dalai Lama

The absolutely most content and happy people I know are those who are spiritual in this world. In my view, spirituality is different from religion. I appreciate and respect the religions of the world, yet to me spirituality is not tied to any religion.

Having a spiritual connection brings joy to our lives. It is a tremendously freeing feeling when we realize that we are more than our bodies and our egos. I find that I feel most connected to God when I am close to nature. If you do too, make it a priority to be in nature on a regular basis.

ACTIVITY: Schedule a time for a hike, bird watching, planting and nurturing flowers, sitting under trees (and plant a few while you are at it), gardening, being with animals, looking at the sky, the stars, and the moon.

When we give from a place of love to others, we are replenishing our own selves and our souls. Some examples of giving from a place of love are helping others such as elderly people at nursing homes, the sick in hospitals, feeding the homeless and distributing baskets at Thanksgiving and Christmas. Another example would be recycling clothes and toys no longer needed to charitable organizations.

"Life's most persistent and urgent question is:
What are you doing for others?"

Martin Luther King, Jr.

Giving of ourselves helps us to feel better and more connected to God. It brings satisfaction, peace of mind, and contentment to our lives. Modeling these behaviors is the most effective and powerful way to teach our children about spirituality.

"Be the change you want
to see in the world."

Gandhi

Reflecting on our own connection to spirituality is vital to being an effective and caring parent. Taking time to meditate reduces the stress in our lives and gives us valuable insights. Meditation often brings us right to the Source. When we are connected to the Source, life can be magical, and even with the problems that occur, you can see the perfection. We become more loving, kind, and at peace with ourselves as we meditate regularly. One meditation CD I highly recommend is "Meditations for Manifesting" by Dr. Wayne Dyer. You can find and purchase this through the website **www.hayhouse.com**. This website also offers self-help and spiritual books by many authors.

"Children have never been good at listening to their elders,
but they have never failed to imitate them."

James Baldwin

Set aside time daily to be thankful and appreciative. Live from that place of love. When we are aligned with the Source and are being authentic, our children feel it. I know that seeking a spiritual connection is of the utmost importance, and when you find it, **your children will benefit greatly**!

There is a list of books and authors that I highly recommend at the end of this book should you want to read some of the books that have brought me great joy and insight.

One of the things you can do to help you stay in this spiritual perspective is to be filled with....

Chapter 27

Gratitude

"Grateful people are happy people."
Greg Young

Every happy person I know has a healthy sense of gratitude. When you are thankful for each gift that life gives to you, it seems like life is glad to give you more gifts. When you focus on what is right about life, you are in a much better position to handle the bumps that will occur.

How do you teach your children to be grateful? Modeling is the most effective teaching method. You can also get into the habit of pointing out things they have to be grateful for. Lou Holtz gives the example of driving his family to the poorest section of town to show them the run down houses in which some people live. Another way is to bring them to a homeless soup kitchen, to a retirement home to visit the elderly, or to the hospital to visit the sick. Have them help with the Special Olympics or adopt a poor, elderly person to give either time and/or money.

These activities will accomplish two things -- helping them to become grateful and also helping them to feel good about helping others.

It is almost impossible to be in a "victim" mode when you are being grateful and looking for the positive. Be thankful for another day of life. Each day provides you with an opportunity to help others and enjoy life.

Being grateful is one of the cornerstones of fully functioning people. What are some other qualities of fully functioning people? They are aware of their blessings, are joyous, laugh easily, and have a good sense of humor. They usually are action oriented, work on the things they wish to change (while accepting things they cannot change). Fully functioning people give back to the universe by helping others, they live in the present (realize they cannot change the past or live in the future), and smile easily and often.

Be grateful! One way of demonstrating gratefulness for your life is to….

Chapter 28

Take Some Time For Yourself

We live in such a fast-paced world. It is easy to get caught up in a whirlwind of activity and responsibilities. Not only do we forget to smell the flowers, we sometimes are going so fast that we do not even see them!

When was the last time you took some time just for you?

If we do not take time to replenish ourselves, it is hard to have much to give to someone else. Taking some time for yourself is one of the best investments you can make for your children's self-esteem. If you do not take the time to nourish yourself, you may begin to feel resentful or stressed out. Eventually, we release this resentment or stress onto our family members.

What do you enjoy doing? Take at least a few minutes each day to do something for yourself. It can be as simple as reading a newspaper, spending a few quiet moments in reflection, taking a walk outside, or making time for a hobby. Listening to soothing music can be very relaxing. I personally love the CD "For

God Alone" by Mark Kelso.   You can find his CDs at the website http://muddyangel.com.

My last recommendation in this area is to do some form of exercise daily. Start small and build up to whatever level you set as a goal. Exercise is a wonderful stress release, gives you a better outlook, and increases your energy level.

ACTIVITY: Decide what would serve to nourish you and what form of exercise you would most enjoy. Make the commitment to begin by tomorrow. Walking is a great form of exercise to consider. It will help for you to have a partner, if possible, for the exercise portion.

One possible way to get some nourishment time is to take advantage of...

Chapter 29

The Magical Influence Of Grandparents

Grandparents have long been providing opportunities for parents to take a break from parenting. Most of the time, grandparents usually come closest to giving true unconditional love to your children. They don't have the responsibility that you have as parents and can provide true acceptance and love to your children like no one else. And they often times have learned from their own mistakes.

During a three-year period when my children were young, we took two vacations a year. One was with the whole family, and one was a snow skiing vacation for my wife and me. On those skiing trips, my mother and father kept our children. They would behave for their grandparents for the whole week, yet the first hour we were back, they would start arguing or fussing about something. My mother would say, "Now, you have been good all week, don't start misbehaving for your mom and dad."

Numerous other times when my parents kept our children, they always seemed to behave and listen to their grandparents. I think that grandparents are usually more at ease with children. They have had more life experiences with which to better handle children. They also realize how precious and special each child is.

NOTE: Your parents paid their dues and are entitled to their freedom. Respect that. Be careful how often you use your parents as babysitters. Make sure to find out what is the right amount for them -- ask them, don't assume. And make sure that they want to watch your children at the time you ask before agreeing to bring them.

There are always exceptions to every rule, but generally, you can't go wrong by letting your children be around their grandparents as much as possible. However, make sure that the grandparents agree to any rules that you have.

I can sum up the difference between being a parent and being a grandparent by this one story. When I was a teenager, my mother told me that when I was born, I had a big nose at birth and when the doctor first showed me to her, she cried. Dr. Fernandez had to console her by telling her that my face would grow and catch up with my nose. She told me this story when I was a teenager, and she also mentioned that I turned out to be a handsome boy.

Fast forward to 1973 when my first son was born. My mom went to look at the babies in the nursery and immediately picked out my son, Gregory, Jr. She was telling everyone that he had a nose just like his father and she could have picked him out of 1,000 babies. She also said he was the cutest baby in the nursery. She didn't cry when she saw my son like she did when she first saw me.

The first time I disciplined one of my children in front of my parents, it really affected them. These tough (though always loving) people who raised me with such discipline and showed no doubt when administering it, could hardly stand to see one of their grandchildren corrected or disciplined. It bothered them so much they said, "I know that they need discipline, but please don't discipline them in front of us."

Grandparents help children feel special by accepting them just as they are. Many grandparents may believe that life is giving them a second chance to correct any mistakes they feel they may have made with their children.

Speaking of making mistakes...

Chapter 30

Admit When You Have Made A Mistake

"An error doesn't become a mistake
until you refuse to correct it."

O. A. Battista

You cannot imagine how much a child will learn from hearing a parent admit when he or she has made a mistake. The first time is the hardest. Once you get into the habit of being honest with yourself and your children, it becomes easier and easier to do. This also works with your spouse, co-workers, and others in your life. You don't lose face by being a person who admits when you have made a mistake; instead, you gain respect!

Once when my older son Greg was about five, I disciplined him for some unacceptable behavior. He was more upset than usual, and when I asked why, he said, "Keith (his younger brother) did the same thing, and you didn't punish him." I asked Greg when Keith did that because I couldn't remember. Greg replied,

"About a year ago." Wow, I thought, I am in trouble. So I apologized for not being consistent and hugged him.

Closely tied to this concept of admitting when you make a mistake is one of being honest with your children. Tell them when you just don't know or when you need time to think about something before deciding. It is better to admit that you don't know something than to mislead them into thinking that you have all the answers. Often times, we will make a better decision if we give it some thought or ask for input from others before making a decision.

Allowing yourself some flexibility can lead you to another vital parenting skill....

Chapter 31

Forgive Yourself For Not Being
A Perfect Parent

"The longer we dwell on our misfortunes,
the greater is their power to harm us."

Voltaire

Just as there are no perfect children, there are no perfect parents. Realize that even if you are doing the best that you know how to do, it still means sometimes making mistakes. Dwelling on past mistakes serves no useful purpose. If we want to handle something differently, then we just need to resolve to do better the next time. **The past is dead!** The only thing that matters is what you do **now** and what you intend to do in the future. As someone once said, "Don't look back unless you want to go that way."

"You can't have a better tomorrow
if you are thinking about
yesterday all the time."

Charles F. Kettering

I remember when I wanted my daughter Rachael to run in a summer track league. My wife saw clearly before I did that although Rachael loved track, she was not thrilled about training all year and running in the heat in Louisiana in the summer. So after checking with Rachael, I found out that her mother was right. I had made a mistake in thinking this was something Rachael wanted, when actually my daughter was doing it to please me. This was one of many mistakes I made, yet I know I made even more good decisions. We all make mistakes, just admit them, correct them if possible, and move on.

By reading this and other books on parenting, you are making an effort to be the best parent you can possibly be. **Parenting is probably one of the most difficult jobs in the world. Being a parent can also be one of the most fulfilling and rewarding jobs in the world!** Taking the time to read this book shows that you are a parent who really cares about your children.

But what if you are not the only parents involved? That leads us to discuss…

Chapter 32

Divorce, Separation And Step Families

I was married for 25 years, and when our youngest child was 20, my wife and I separated. Two years later we were divorced, and she remarried. During a divorce, keeping a relationship from becoming bitter is not an easy task because there is always pain involved in dissolving a relationship.

In our divorce process, there were challenges to maintaining a good relationship, yet we managed to take two family vacations together while we were separated. We also spent the Christmas holidays and other times together. I made it a priority to get along with my ex-wife's new husband. Even though our children were adults, I realized that they would always want their parents together. Though that is not probable in the sense of remarrying each other, we can still give them the pleasure of enjoying our company without blaming each other or fighting.

We are conscious not to put our children in the middle of our issues. One example is that we agree on when the children will visit each of us on holidays and other special events. We give and take both ways, and we consult with our children. It is important to keep your focus on finding ways to make things work smoothly and avoid putting the children in conflict.

Two important questions to ask yourself are:

- What is best for our children?
- What good qualities of my ex-spouse can I remember, focus on, and appreciate in their presence?

When younger children are involved with a stepparent, some guidelines are helpful.

1. As a couple, you need to communicate and establish the "house rules." Once you agree to them, it is important that both parents stick to them and are consistent in applying any discipline. If something needs changing, consult your partner first and jointly declare the new policy. Be aware that children are masters at getting parents into conflict if they are not aware of what is happening.

2. As the parent, make sure to support your spouse (the stepparent). Also, as the stepparent, don't try to "give in" to win the children's favor and make the parent the "bad guy."

3. As a stepparent, be aware there is probably some resentment towards you. Be patient in winning the trust of each child. Especially at first, allow the parent to do most of the disciplining. Take time to talk to each child and develop a relationship.

This subject could require much more that these simple thoughts. If you find yourself needing more information, go to the bookstore and find a book that focuses only on this subject.

And it is finally time for...

Chapter 33

Closing Thoughts

*"The most precious thing a parent can give a child
is a lifetime of happy memories."*

Frank Tyger

Below is a **Parent's Creed** for you to read and review often:

1. I listen attentively to my children.
2. I hug my children at **least** once every day.
3. I tell my children that I love them every day.
4. I believe in my children, and express that belief to them as often as possible. I want them to feel like they can do anything they put their minds to. **I am on their side!**
5. I spend at least 15 minutes per week alone with each child.
6. I respect my children's right to privacy.
7. I realize that my child is a **whole** person. Even though their bodies may be small, their feelings are just as big as adults' feelings.
8. I admit to them when I make a mistake.
9. I provide consistent discipline **with love**.
10. I separate the behavior from the child. I always speak positively about the person. If corrections are needed, I speak about the undesirable behavior.
11. I accept the differences in my children and appreciate each one's uniqueness. I accept them just as they are.
12. I encourage my children to be participants and not just spectators in the adventure of life.
13. I forgive myself for not being a perfect parent and realize that I cannot change the past. I learn from any mistakes that I might make and do things differently the next time. As a parent, I model living in the present.
14. I nurture my spiritual connection, and I recognize that my relationship with my children is a reflection of my spiritual awareness.

I want to leave you with some messages:

- There are two states of being, love and fear. Whatever is not love is fear, so stay in love.

- Your awareness is such a gift to your children and to everyone. So cultivate awareness.

- Children are treasures from God. Always hold children in respect. Have a respect for all life.

- Surrender can be a good word…accept the perfection of this moment. In doing so, spiritual solutions often appear to life's difficulties.

Learn to love yourself more,
For the more you are able to love yourself,
The more love you have to give away!

As the author, I want to **thank you** for reading this book! And please, if you enjoyed it, recommend it to your friends.

Good luck in your role as a parent, and please enjoy the journey.

Recommended Books

Dan Millman
- *The Laws of Spirit*
- *Way of The Peaceful Warrior*
- *Sacred Journey of the Peaceful Warrior*
- *No Ordinary Moments*

Og Mandino
- *The Greatest Salesman In The World*
- *The Choice*
- *The Greatest Miracle In The World*
- *Mission Success*
- *The Greatest Secret In The World*
- *The Christ Commission*
- *The Return of The Ragpicker*

Wayne Dyer
- *There's a Spiritual Solution to Every Problem*
- *Wisdom of the Ages*
- *Your Sacred Self*

Don Miguel Ruiz
- *The Four Agreements*
- *The Mastery of Love*

James Redfield
- *The Celestine Prophecy*
- *The Secret of Shambhala*

Neale Donald Walsch
- *The New Revelations: A Conversation with God*
- *Bringers of the Light*

Greg is a member of the National Speakers Association and is available for speaking engagements and workshops for parents and for students. You or your friends can purchase this book and other products at his website listed below.

Greg would be glad to address any questions you may have on parenting. Just send him an email to the email address below.

Contact Information:
Greg Young:
P. O. Box 67
Centerville, Louisiana 70522-0067
Email: greg.young@cox-internet.com
Website: www.Parents4SelfEsteem.com
Phone: 337-829-9800